To

_____

From

_____

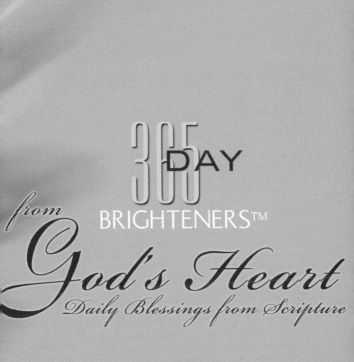

365 DAY BRIGHTENERS™

from

God's Heart

Daily Blessings from Scripture

365 Day Brighteners™ from God's Heart:
Copyright © 2004 DaySpring® Cards, Inc.
Published by Garborg's®, a brand of DaySpring® Cards, Inc.
Siloam Springs, Arkansas
www.dayspring.com

Design by Moe Studio

Scripture quotations are from the following sources: The HOLY BIBLE, NEW INTERNATIONAL VERSION® (NIV)® © 1973, 1978, 1984 by International Bible Society. Used by permission of Zondervan Publishing House. The Holy Bible, New Century Version (NCV) © 1987, 1988, 1991 by Word Publishing, Dallas, Texas 75039. Used by permission. THE MESSAGE © Eugene H. Peterson 1993, 1994, 1995. Used by permission of NavPress Publishing Group. All rights reserved. The Living Bible (TLB) © 1971 by permission of Tyndale House Publishers, Inc., Wheaton, IL. The Holy Bible, New Living Translation (NLT) © 1996 by permission of Tyndale House Publishers, Inc., Wheaton, IL. The NEW AMERICAN STANDARD BIBLE® (NASB) © The Lockman Foundation 1960, 1962, 1963, 1968, 1971, 1972, 1973, 1975, 1977, 1995. Used by permission. (www.Lockman.org). The New King James Version (NKJV) © 1982, Thomas Nelson, Inc. The New Revised Standard Version of the Bible (NRSV) © 1989 Division of Christian Education, National Council of Churches. Used by permission of Zondervan Publishing House.

ISBN 1-58061-787-5
Printed in China

365 DAY BRIGHTENERS™

BRIGHTENERS™

from

God's Heart

Daily Blessings from Scripture

Our God gives you everything you need, makes you everything you're to be.... Your faith is growing phenomenally; your love for each other is developing wonderfully. Why, it's only right that we give thanks. We're so proud of you; you're so steady and determined in your faith.

2 THESSALONIANS 1:2-4 THE MESSAGE

January 1

We know that in all things God works
for the good of those who love him,
who have been called according to his purpose.

ROMANS 8:28 NIV

January 2

$\mathcal{L}$ater, in one of his talks, Jesus said to the people, "I am the Light of the world. So if you follow me, you won't be stumbling through the darkness, for living light will flood your path."

JOHN 8:12 TLB

January 3

Delight yourself in the Lord and he will give you the desires of your heart. Commit your way to the Lord; trust in him and he will do this: He will make your righteousness shine like the dawn, the justice of your cause like the noonday sun.

PSALM 37:4-6 NIV

January 4

I am the Gate. Anyone who goes through me will be cared for—will freely go in and out, and find pasture. A thief is only there to steal and kill and destroy. I came so they can have real and eternal life, more and better life than they ever dreamed of. I am the Good Shepherd. The Good Shepherd puts the sheep before himself, sacrifices himself if necessary.

JOHN 10:9-11 THE MESSAGE

January 5

Pray without ceasing; in everything give thanks; for this is God's will for you in Christ Jesus.

1 THESSALONIANS 5:17-18 NASB

January 6

"Be still and know that I am God; I will be exalted among the nations; I will be exalted in the earth." The Lord Almighty is with us; the God of Jacob is our fortress.

PSALM 46:10-11 NIV

January 7

Then the word of the Lord came to Jeremiah, saying, "Behold, I am the Lord, the God of all flesh. Is there anything too hard for Me?"

JEREMIAH 32:26-27 NKJV

January 8

Trust in the Lord with all your heart
and lean not on your own understanding; in all your
ways acknowledge him, and he will make
your paths straight.

PROVERBS 3:5-6 NIV

January 9

Let your conduct be without covetousness; be content with such things as you have. For He Himself has said, "I will never leave you nor forsake you."

HEBREWS 13:5 NKJV

January 10

*T*hose who trust in the Lord are like Mount Zion, which cannot be shaken but endures forever. As the mountains surround Jerusalem, so the Lord surrounds his people both now and forevermore.

PSALM 125:1-2 NIV

January 11

*F*ear not, for I am with you. Do not be dismayed. I am your God. I will strengthen you; I will help you; I will uphold you with my victorious right hand.

ISAIAH 41:10 TLB

January 12

And we, who with unveiled faces all reflect the Lord's glory, are being transformed into his likeness with ever-increasing glory, which comes from the Lord, who is the Spirit.

2 CORINTHIANS 3:18 NIV

January 13

$\mathcal{D}$raw near to God and He will draw near to you.... Humble yourselves in the sight of the Lord, and He will lift you up.

JAMES 4:8,10 NKJV

January 14

He who dwells in the shelter of the Most High will rest in the shadow of the Almighty. I will say of the Lord, "He is my refuge and my fortress, my God, in whom I trust."

PSALM 91:1-2 NIV

January 15

The boundary lines have fallen for me in pleasant places; surely I have a delightful inheritance. I will praise the Lord who counsels me; even at night my heart instructs me. I have set the Lord always before me. Because he is at my right hand, I will not be shaken.

PSALM 16:6-8 NIV

January 16

*H*e told his disciples, "I have been given all authority in heaven and earth. Therefore go and make disciples in all the nations, baptizing them into the name of the Father and of the Son and of the Holy Spirit."

MATTHEW 28:18-19 TLB

January 17

"For I know the plans that I have for you," declares the Lord, "plans for welfare and not for calamity to give you a future and a hope."

JEREMIAH 29:11 NASB

January 18

*F*orgetting what is behind and straining toward what is ahead, I press on toward the goal to win the prize for which God has called me heavenward in Christ Jesus.

PHILIPPIANS 3:13-14 NIV

January 19

And whatever we ask we receive from Him, because we keep His commandments and do those things that are pleasing in His sight. And this is His commandment: that we should believe on the name of His Son Jesus Christ and love one another, as He gave us commandment.

1 JOHN 3:22-23 NKJV

January 20

*O*ne thing God has spoken, two things have I
heard: that you, O God, are strong, and that you,
O Lord, are loving. Surely you will reward each
person according to what he has done.

PSALM 62:11-12 NIV

January 21

*B*ut there is forgiveness with Thee, that Thou mayest be feared. I wait for the Lord, my soul does wait, and in His word do I hope. My soul waits for the Lord more than the watchmen for the morning; indeed, more than the watchmen for the morning.

PSALM 130:4-6 NASB

January 22

*B*e still before the Lord and wait patiently for him; do not fret when men succeed in their ways, when they carry out their wicked schemes. Refrain from anger and turn from wrath; do not fret— it leads only to evil.

PSALM 37:7-8 NIV

January 23

$\mathcal{W}$e were therefore buried with him through baptism into death in order that, just as Christ was raised from the dead through the glory of the Father, we too may live a new life. If we have been united with him like this in his death, we will certainly also be united with him in his resurrection.

ROMANS 6:4–5 NIV

January 24

There is far more to your life than the food you put in your stomach, more to your outer appearance than the clothes you hang on your body. Look at the birds, free and unfettered, not tied down to a job description, careless in the care of God. And you count far more to him than birds.

MATTHEW 6:25-26 THE MESSAGE

January 25

*H*ear my cry, O God; listen to my prayer. From the ends of the earth I call to you, I call as my heart grows faint; lead me to the rock that is higher than I. For you have been my refuge, a strong tower against the foe.

PSALM 61:1-3 NIV

January 26

Wait for the Lord, and keep His way, and He will exalt you to inherit the land.

PSALM 37:34 NASB

January 27

Those who are led by the Spirit of God are sons of God. For you did not receive a spirit that makes you a slave again to fear, but you received the Spirit of sonship. And by him we cry, "Abba, Father."

ROMANS 8:14–15 NIV

January 28

$\mathcal{A}$nd let us not get tired of doing what is right,
for after a while we will reap a harvest of blessing
if we don't get discouraged and give up. That's
why whenever we can we should always be
kind to everyone, and especially to our
Christian brothers.

GALATIANS 6:9-10 TLB

January 29

But it is the spirit in a man, the breath of the Almighty, that gives him understanding.

JOB 32:8 NIV

January 30

Praise the Lord! Praise, O servants of the Lord,
Praise the name of the Lord! Blessed be the name
of the Lord from this time forth and forevermore!
From the rising of the sun to its going down the
Lord's name is to be praised.

PSALM 113:1-3 NKJV

January 31

I will bless the Lord who counsels me; he gives me wisdom in the night. He tells me what to do. I am always thinking of the Lord; and because he is so near, I never need to stumble or to fall. Heart, body, and soul are filled with joy.

PSALM 16:7-9 TLB

February 1

*A*bove all else, guard your heart, for it is the wellspring of life.... Let your eyes look straight ahead, fix your gaze directly before you. Make level paths for your feet and take only ways that are firm.

PROVERBS 4:23,25-26 NIV

February 2

The steps of a man are established by the Lord;
and He delights in his way. When he falls, he
shall not be hurled headlong; because the Lord
is the One who holds his hand.

PSALM 37:23-24 NASB

February 3

This day is holy to our Lord. Do not sorrow, for the joy of the Lord is your strength.

NEHEMIAH 8:10 NKJV

February 4

So here's what I want you to do, God helping you: Take your everyday, ordinary life—your sleeping, eating, going-to-work, and walking-around life— and place it before God as an offering. Embracing what God does for you is the best thing you can do for him. Don't become so well-adjusted to your culture that you fit into it without even thinking. Instead, fix your attention on God. You'll be changed from the inside out.

ROMANS 12:1-2 THE MESSAGE

February 5

$\mathcal{N}$o temptation has seized you except what is common to man. And God is faithful; he will not let you be tempted beyond what you can bear. But when you are tempted, he will also provide a way out so that you can stand up under it.

1 CORINTHIANS 10:13 NIV

February 6

*E*very good and perfect gift is from above,
coming down from the Father of the heavenly lights,
who does not change like shifting shadows.

JAMES 1:17 NIV

February 7

I will go before you and will level the mountains;
I will break down gates of bronze and cut through
bars of iron. I will give you the treasures of darkness,
riches stored in secret places, so that you may know
that I am the Lord, the God of Israel
who summons you by name.

ISAIAH 45:2-3 NIV

February 8

O Lord, Thou hast searched me and known me.
Thou dost know when I sit down and when I rise up;
Thou dost understand my thought from afar.

PSALM 139:1-2 NASB

February 9

He will cover you with his feathers, and under his wings you will find refuge; his faithfulness will be your shield and rampart. You will not fear the terror of night, nor the arrow that flies by day.

PSALM 91:4-5 NIV

February 10

Therefore the Lord will wait, that He may be gracious to you; and therefore He will be exalted, that He may have mercy on you. For the Lord is a God of justice; blessed are all those who wait for Him. For the people shall dwell in Zion at Jerusalem; you shall weep no more. He will be very gracious to you at the sound of your cry; when He hears it, He will answer you.

ISAIAH 30:18-19 NKJV

February 11

$\mathcal{B}$ut for you who fear my name, the Sun of Righteousness will rise with healing in his wings. And you will go free, leaping with joy like calves let out to pasture.

MALACHI 4:2 TLB

February 12

I will come and proclaim your mighty acts,
O sovereign Lord; I will proclaim your righteousness,
yours alone. Since my youth, O God, you
have taught me, and to this day I
declare your marvelous deeds.

PSALM 71:16-17 NIV

February 13

The person who knows my commandments and keeps them, that's who loves me. And the person who loves me will be loved by my Father, and I will love him and make myself plain to him.

JOHN 14:21 THE MESSAGE

February 14

If you have faith as small as a mustard seed, you can say to this mulberry tree, "Be uprooted and planted in the sea," and it will obey you.

LUKE 17:6 NIV

February 15

*B*ehold, I stand at the door and knock. If anyone hears My voice and opens the door, I will come in to him and dine with him, and he with Me.

REVELATION 3:20 NKJV

February 16

The righteous cry and the Lord hears,
and delivers them out of all their troubles.

PSALM 34:17 NASB

February 17

$\mathcal{L}$ive in me. Make your home in me just as I do
in you. In the same way that a branch can't
bear grapes by itself but only by being joined
to the vine, you can't bear fruit unless you
are joined with me.

JOHN 15:4 THE MESSAGE

February 18

If anyone would come after me, he must deny himself and take up his cross daily and follow me. For whoever wants to save his life will lose it but whoever loses his life for me will save it.

LUKE 9:23-24 NIV

February 19

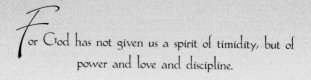

*F*or God has not given us a spirit of timidity, but of power and love and discipline.

2 TIMOTHY 1:7 NASB

February 20

Let them shout for joy and be glad, who favor my righteous cause; and let them say continually, "Let the Lord be magnified, who has pleasure in the prosperity of His servant." And my tongue shall speak of Your righteousness and of Your praise all the day long.

PSALM 35:27-28 NKJV

February 21

The heavens are telling the glory of God; they are a marvelous display of his craftsmanship. Day and night they keep on telling about God. Without a sound or word, silent in the skies, their message reaches out to all the world. The sun lives in the heavens where God placed it

PSALM 19:1-3 TLB

February 22

But seek first his kingdom and his righteousness, and all these things will be given to you as well. Therefore do not worry about tomorrow, for tomorrow will worry about itself.

MATTHEW 6:33-34 NIV

February 23

$\mathcal{M}$y response is to get down on my knees before the Father. I ask him to strengthen you by his Spirit—not a brute strength but a glorious inner strength—that Christ will live in you as you open the door and invite him in. And I ask him that with both feet planted firmly on love, you'll be able to take in with all Christians the extravagant dimensions of Christ's love. Reach out and experience the breadth! Test its length! Plumb the depths! Rise to the heights! Live full lives, full in the fullness of God.

EPHESIANS 3:14,16-19 THE MESSAGE

February 24

$\mathcal{P}$raise the Lord, O my soul, and forget not all his benefits—who redeems your life from the pit and crowns you with love and compassion, who satisfies your desires with good things so that your youth is renewed like the eagle's.

PSALM 103:2,4-5 NIV

February 25

For thus said the Lord God, the Holy One of Israel: In returning and rest you shall be saved; in quietness and in trust shall be your strength.

ISAIAH 30:15 NRSV

February 26

*F*inally, brothers, whatever is true, whatever is noble, whatever is right, whatever is pure, whatever is lovely, whatever is admirable—if anything is excellent or praiseworthy—think about such things.

PHILIPPIANS 4:8 NIV

February 27

*T*his book of the law shall not depart from your mouth, but you shall meditate on it day and night, so that you may be careful to do according to all that is written in it; for then you will make your way prosperous, and then you will have success.

JOSHUA 1:8 NASB

February 28

Some trust in chariots and some in horses,
but we trust in the name of the Lord our God.
They are brought to their knees and fall, but we
rise up and stand firm.

PSALM 20:7-8 NIV

February 29

$\mathcal{O}$ur God gives you everything you need,
makes you everything you're to be.

2 THESSALONIANS 1:2 THE MESSAGE

March 1

"Then you will call upon me and come and pray to me, and I will listen to you. You will seek me and find me when you seek me with all your heart. I will be found by you," declares the Lord.

JEREMIAH 29:12-14 NIV

March 2

God sees not as man sees, for man looks at the outward appearance, but the Lord looks at the heart.

1 SAMUEL 16:7 NASB

March 3

*I*n solemn truth I tell you, anyone believing in me shall do the same miracles I have done, and even greater ones, because I am going to be with the Father. You can ask him for anything, using my name, and I will do it, for this will bring praise to the Father because of what I, the Son, will do for you.

JOHN 14:12-13 TLB

March 4

Rejoice in the Lord always. Again I will say, rejoice! Let your gentleness be known to all men. The Lord is at hand. Be anxious for nothing, but in everything by prayer and supplication, with thanksgiving, let your requests be made known to God.

PHILIPPIANS 4:4-6 NKJV

March 5

There remains therefore a Sabbath rest for the people of God. For the one who has entered His rest has himself also rested from his works, as God did from His. Let us therefore be diligent to enter that rest, lest anyone fall through following the same example of disobedience.

HEBREWS 4:9-11 NASB

March 6

Whether you turn to the right or to the left, your ears will hear a voice behind you, saying, "This is the way; walk in it."

ISAIAH 30:21 NIV

March 7

$\mathcal{A}$nd He said to me, "My grace is sufficient for you, for My strength is made perfect in weakness." Therefore most gladly I will rather boast in my infirmities, that the power of Christ may rest upon me. Therefore I take pleasure in infirmities, in reproaches, in needs, in persecutions, in distresses, for Christ's sake. For when I am weak, then I am strong.

2 CORINTHIANS 12:9-10 NKJV

March 8

$\mathcal{W}$hatever I have, wherever I am, I can make it through anything in the One who makes me who I am.

PHILIPPIANS 4:13 THE MESSAGE

March 9

To the Jews who had believed him, Jesus said,
"If you hold to my teaching, you are really my
disciples. Then you will know the truth, and
the truth will set you free."

JOHN 8:31-32 NIV

March 10

For we do not have a High Priest who cannot sympathize with our weaknesses, but was in all points tempted as we are, yet without sin.

HEBREWS 4:15 NKJV

March 11

$\mathcal{W}$orship the Lord with gladness; come into his presence with singing. Know that the Lord is God. It is he that made us, and we are his; we are his people, and the sheep of his pasture. Enter his gates with thanksgiving, and his courts with praise. Give thanks to him, bless his name.

PSALM 100:2-4 NRSV

March 12

My sheep listen to my voice; I know them, and they follow me. I give them eternal life, and they shall never perish; no one can snatch them out of my hand. My Father, who has given them to me, is greater than all; no one can snatch them out of my Father's hand.

JOHN 10:27-29 NIV

March 13

"*Now* therefore, I pray, if I have found grace in Your sight, show me now Your way, that I may know You and that I may find grace in Your sight". And He said, "My Presence will go with you, and I will give you rest."

EXODUS 33:13-14 NKJV

March 14

So I say to you, Ask, and it will be given you; search, and you will find; knock, and the door will be opened for you. For everyone who asks receives, and everyone who searches finds, and for everyone who knocks, the door will be opened.

LUKE 11:9-10 NRSV

March 15

God made the heavens—Royal splendor radiates
from him, a powerful beauty sets him apart.

PSALM 96:5,6 THE MESSAGE

March 16

"For my thoughts are not your thoughts, neither are your ways my ways," declares the Lord. "As the heavens are higher than the earth, so are my ways higher than your ways and my thoughts than your thoughts."

ISAIAH 55:8-9 NIV

March 17

$\mathcal{B}$e kind to each other, tenderhearted, forgiving one another, just as God has forgiven you because you belong to Christ.

EPHESIANS 4:32 TLB

March 18

*H*appy are those who do not follow the advice
of the wicked, or take the path that sinners tread, or
sit in the seat of scoffers; but their delight is in the law
of the Lord, and on his law they meditate
day and night.

PSALM 1:1-2 NRSV

March 19

*T*he Lord bless you and keep you; the Lord make his face shine upon you and be gracious to you; the Lord turn his face toward you and give you peace.

NUMBERS 6:24-26 NIV

March 20

We know it so well we've embraced it heart and soul this love that comes from God. God is love. When we take up permanent residence in a life of love, we live in God and God lives in us.

1 JOHN 4:16 THE MESSAGE

March 21

*Bless the Lord, O my soul; and all that
is within me, bless His holy name! Bless the Lord,
O my soul, and forget not all His benefits: who
forgives all your iniquities, who heals all your diseases.*

PSALM 103:1-3 NKJV

March 22

Answer me when I call to you, O my righteous God. Give me relief from my distress; be merciful to me and hear my prayer.

PSALM 4:1 NIV

March 23

There is no fear in love; but perfect love casts out fear, because fear involves punishment, and the one who fears is not perfected in love.

1 JOHN 4:18 NASB

March 24

*B*e energetic in your life of salvation, reverent and sensitive before God. That energy is God's energy, an energy deep within you, God himself willing and working at what will give him the most pleasure.

PHILIPPIANS 2:12-13 THE MESSAGE

March 25

*Y*ou hem me in—behind and before; you have laid

your hand upon me. Such knowledge is too wonderful

for me, lofty for me to attain.

PSALM 139:5-6 NIV

March 26

If you will humble yourselves under the mighty hand of God, in his good time he will lift you up.

1 PETER 5:6 TLB

March 27

This is what the Lord says: "Stand at the crossroads and look; ask for the ancient paths, ask where the good way is, and walk in it, and you will find rest for your souls."

JEREMIAH 6:16 NIV

March 28

But Thou, O Lord, art a shield about me, my glory, and the One who lifts my head. I was crying to the Lord with my voice, and He answered me from His holy mountain. I lay down and slept; I awoke, for the Lord sustains me.

PSALM 3:3–5 NASB

March 29

*W*hen two of you get together on anything
at all on earth and make a prayer of it,
my Father in heaven goes into action.

MATTHEW 18:19 THE MESSAGE

March 30

*O*ur Father in heaven, Hallowed be Your name. Your kingdom come. Your will be done on earth as it is in heaven. Give us this day our daily bread.

MATTHEW 6:9-11 NKJV

March 31

There is no one like the God of Jeshurun, who rides on the heavens to help you and on the clouds in his majesty. The eternal God is your refuge, and underneath are the everlasting arms.

DEUTERONOMY 33:26-27 NIV

April 1

So I tell you, whatever you ask for in prayer,
believe that you have received it, and it will be yours.

MARK 11:24 NRSV

April 2

I will not be afraid of ten thousands of people who have set themselves against me all around. Arise, O Lord; save me, O my God! Salvation belongs to the Lord. Your blessing is upon Your people.

PSALM 3:6-8 NKJV

April 3

*H*is love endures forever. To the One who
remembered us in our low estate. His love endures
forever. And freed us from our enemies,
his love endures forever.

Psalm 136:22-24 NIV

April 4

Not that we are adequate in ourselves to consider anything as coming from ourselves, but our adequacy is from God.

2 CORINTHIANS 3:5 NASB

April 5

If you have faith as small as a mustard seed, you can say to this mountain, "Move from here to there" and it will move. Nothing will be impossible for you.

MATTHEW 17:20 NIV

April 6

The true Bread is a Person—the one sent by God
from heaven, and he gives life to the world.

JOHN 6:33 TLB

April 7

$\mathcal{D}$on't fuss about what's on the table at mealtimes or if the clothes in your closet are in fashion. There is far more to your inner life than the food you put in your stomach, more to your outer appearance than the clothes you hang on your body.

LUKE 12:22-23 THE MESSAGE

April 8

So then, just as you received Christ Jesus
as Lord, continue to live in him, rooted and built up
in him, strengthened in the faith as you were taught
and overflowing with thankfulness.

COLOSSIANS 2:6-7 NIV

April 9

*F*or lo, the winter is past, the rain is over and gone. The flowers appear on the earth; the time of singing has come, and the voice of the turtledove is heard in our land.

SONG OF SOLOMON 2:11-12 NKJV

April 10

Indeed, I have been crucified with Christ. My ego is no longer central. It is no longer important that I appear righteous before you or have your good opinion, and I am no longer driven to impress God. Christ lives in me. The life you see me living is not "mine," but it is lived by faith in the Son of God, who loved me and gave himself for me.

GALATIANS 2:20 THE MESSAGE

April 11

And after the wind an earthquake, but the Lord was not in the earthquake. And after the earthquake a fire, but the Lord was not in the fire; and after the fire a sound of a gentle blowing.

1 KINGS 19:11-12 NASB

April 12

Can a mother forget the baby at her breast
and have no compassion on the child she has borne?
Though she may forget, I will not forget you!
See, I have engraved you on the palms of my hands;
your walls are ever before me.

ISAIAH 49:15-16 NIV

April 13

$\mathcal{Y}$ou can be sure that God will take care of everything you need, his generosity exceeding even yours in
the glory that pours from Jesus.

PHILIPPIANS 4:19 THE MESSAGE

April 14

For God so loved the world that He gave His only begotten Son, that whoever believes in Him should not perish but have everlasting life.

JOHN 3:16 NKJV

April 15

$\mathcal{M}$ay the favor of the Lord our God rest upon us; establish the work of our hands for us— yes, establish the work of our hands.

PSALM 90:17 NIV

April 16

I have said this to you, so that in me you may have peace. In the world you face persecution. But take courage; I have conquered the world!

JOHN 16:33 NRSV

April 17

I will lift up my eyes to the mountains; from whence shall my help come? My help comes from the Lord, who made heaven and earth.

PSALM 121:1-2 NASB

April 18

*W*alk with me and work with me—watch how I do it. Learn the unforced rhythms of grace. I won't lay anything heavy or ill-fitting on you. Keep company with me and you'll learn to live freely and lightly.

MATTHEW 11:29-30 THE MESSAGE

April 19

So now, since we have been made right in God's sight by faith in his promises, we can have real peace with him because of what Jesus Christ our Lord has done for us. For because of our faith, he has brought us into this place of highest privilege where we now stand, and we confidently and joyfully look forward to actually becoming all that God has had in mind for us to be.

ROMANS 5:1-2 TLB

April 20

There is therefore now no condemnation to those who are in Christ Jesus, who do not walk according to the flesh, but according to the Spirit.

ROMANS 8:1 NKJV

April 21

Give ear to my words, O Lord, consider my sighing. Listen to my cry for help, my King and my God, for to you I pray. In the morning, O Lord, you hear my voice; in the morning I lay my requests before you and wait in expectation.

PSALM 5:1-3 NIV

April 22

*H*e who keeps Israel will neither slumber nor sleep. The Lord is your keeper; the Lord is your shade at your right hand.

PSALM 121:4-5 NRSV

April 23

There has never been the slightest doubt in my mind that the God who started this great work in you would keep at it and bring it to a flourishing finish on the very day Christ Jesus appears.

PHILIPPIANS 1:6 THE MESSAGE

April 24

You are my hiding place; you will protect me from trouble and surround me with songs of deliverance.

PSALM 32:7 NIV

April 25

The Lord is my shepherd; I shall not want.
He makes me to lie down in green pastures;
He leads me beside the still waters.

PSALM 23:1-2 NKJV

April 26

So let us know, let us press on to know the Lord. His going forth is as certain as the dawn; and He will come to us like the rain, like the spring rain watering the earth.

HOSEA 6:3 NASB

April 27

*W*hen a man's ways are pleasing to the Lord,
He makes even his enemies to be at peace with him.
Better is a little with righteousness than great income
with injustice. The mind of man plans his way,
but the Lord directs his steps.

PROVERBS 16:7-9 NASB

April 28

I will set My tabernacle among you, and My soul shall not abhor you. I will walk among you and be your God, and you shall be My people.

LEVITICUS 26:11-12 NKJV

April 29

A word aptly spoken is like apples of gold in settings of silver. Like an earring of gold or an ornament of fine gold is a wise man's rebuke to a listening ear.

PROVERBS 25:11-12 NIV

April 30

God didn't go to all the trouble of sending his Son merely to point an accusing finger, telling the world how bad it was. He came to help, to put the world right again.

JOHN 3:17 THE MESSAGE

May 1

*H*ow great is your goodness, which you have stored up for those who fear you, which you bestow in the sight of men on those who take refuge in you.

PSALM 31:19 NIV

May 2

$\mathcal{J}$esus replied that people soon became thirsty again after drinking this water. "But the water I give them," he said, "becomes a perpetual spring within them, watering them forever with eternal life."

JOHN 4:13-14 TLB

May 3

We give thanks to You, O God, we give thanks! For Your wondrous works declare that Your name is near.

PSALM 75:1 NKJV

May 4

*F*or you shall go out in joy, and be led back in peace; the mountains and the hills before you shall burst into song, and all the trees of the field shall clap their hands.

ISAIAH 55:12 NRSV

May 5

Therefore, if anyone is in Christ, he is a new creation; the old has gone, the new has come!

2 CORINTHIANS 5:17 NIV

May 6

The Lord God is my strength, and He has made my feet like hinds' feet, and makes me walk on my high places.

HABAKKUK 3:19 NASB

May 7

In God, whose word I praise, in the Lord, whose word I praise, in God I trust; I am not afraid. What can a mere mortal do to me?

PSALM 56:10-11 NRSV

May 8

If any of you wants to serve me, then follow me. Then you'll be where I am, ready to serve at a moment's notice. The Father will honor and reward anyone who serves me.

May 9

The name of the Lord is a strong tower;
the righteous run to it and are safe.

PROVERBS 18:10 NIV

May 10

$\mathcal{A}$nd do not be conformed to this world,
but be transformed by the renewing of your mind,
that you may prove what is that good and acceptable
and perfect will of God.

ROMANS 12:2 NKVJ

May 11

I have loved you even as the Father has loved me.
Live within my love. When you obey me you are
living in my love, just as I obey my Father and
live in his love.

JOHN 15:9-10 TLB

May 12

You have made known to me the path of life; you will fill me with joy in your presence, with eternal pleasures at your right hand.

PSALM 16:11 NIV

May 13

Know this: God is God, and God, God. He made us; we didn't make him. We're his people, his well-tended sheep.. For God is sheer beauty, all-generous in love, loyal always and ever.

PSALM 100:3-5 THE MESSAGE

May 14

One thing I asked of the Lord, that will I seek after: to live in the house of the Lord all the days of my life, to behold the beauty of the Lord, and to inquire in his temple. For he will hide me in his shelter in the day of trouble; he will conceal me under the cover of his tent; he will set me high on a rock.

PSALM 27:4-5 NRSV

May 15

*A*sk the Lord for rain in the springtime; it is the Lord who makes the storm clouds. He gives showers of rain to men, and plants of the field to everyone.

ZECHARIAH 10:1 NIV

May 16

*A*nd we are sure of this, that he will listen to us whenever we ask him for anything in line with his will. And if we really know he is listening when we talk to him and make our requests, then we can be sure that he will answer us.

1 JOHN 5:14–15 TLB

May 17

I seek you with all my heart; do not let me stray from your commands. I have hidden your word in my heart that I might not sin against you. Praise be to you, O Lord; teach me your decrees.

PSALM 119:10-12 NIV

May 18

Why are you cast down, O my soul, and why are you disquieted within me? Hope in God; for I shall again praise him, my help and my God.

PSALM 43:5 NRSV

May 19

In the same way, let your light shine before men,
that they may see your good deeds and praise your
Father in heaven.

MATTHEW 5:16 NIV

May 20

He restores my soul. He guides me in paths of righteousness for his name's sake. Even though I walk through the valley of the shadow of death, I will fear no evil, for you are with me; your rod and your staff, they comfort me.

PSALM 23:3-4 NIV

May 21

*W*hatever your task, put yourselves into it,
as done for the Lord and not for your masters, since
you know that from the Lord you will receive the
inheritance as your reward; you serve the Lord Christ.

COLOSSIANS 3:23-24 NRSV

May 22

If you abide in Me, and My words abide in you, ask whatever you wish, and it shall be done for you. By this is My Father glorified, that you bear much fruit, and so prove to be My disciples.

JOHN 15:7-8 NASB

May 23

This is the gate of the Lord, through which the righteous shall enter. I will praise You, for You have answered me, and have become my salvation. This is the day the Lord has made; we will rejoice and be glad in it.

PSALM 118:20-21,24 NKJV

May 24

From one man he made every nation of men, that they should inhabit the whole earth; and he determined the times set for them and the exact places where they should live. God did this so that men would seek him and perhaps reach out for him and find him, though he is not far from each one of us. "For in him we live and move and have our being."

ACTS 17:26-28 NIV

May 25

Those who hope in the Lord will renew their strength. They will soar on wings like eagles; they will run and not grow weary, they will walk and not be faint.

ISAIAH 40:31 NIV

May 26

Some give freely, yet grow all the richer;
others withhold what is due, and only suffer want.
A generous person will be enriched, and one
who gives water will get water.

PROVERBS 11:24–25 NRSV

May 27

But I will always trust in you and in your mercy and shall rejoice in your salvation. I will sing to the Lord because he has blessed me so richly.

PSALM 13:5-6 TLB

May 28

*T*aste and see that the Lord is good; blessed is the man who takes refuge in him. Fear the Lord, you his saints, for those who fear him lack nothing.

PSALM 34:8-9 NIV

May 29

"Behold, I am with you and will keep you wherever you go.... For I will not leave you until I have done what I have spoken to you." Then Jacob awoke from his sleep and said, "Surely the Lord is in this place, and I did not know it."

GENESIS 28:15-16 NKJV

May 30

What marvelous love the Father has extended to us! Just look at it—we're called children of God! That's who we really are.

1 John 3:1 THE MESSAGE

May 31

So we fix our eyes not on what is seen,
but on what is unseen. For what is seen is temporary,
but what is unseen is eternal.

2 CORINTHIANS 4:18 NIV

June 1

$\mathcal{N}$ot unto us, O Lord, not unto us, but to Your name give glory, because of Your mercy, because of Your truth.

PSALM 115:1 NKJV

June 2

The sheep listen to his voice. He calls his own sheep by name and leads them out. When he has brought out all his own, he goes on ahead of them, and his sheep follow him because they know his voice.

JOHN 10:3-4 NIV

June 3

Gracious is the Lord, and righteous; our God is merciful. The Lord protects the simple; when I was brought low, he saved me. Return, O my soul, to your rest, for the Lord has dealt bountifully with you.

PSALM 116:5-7 NRSV

June 4

For the Lord God is a sun and shield; the Lord
bestows favor and honor; no good thing does
he withhold from those whose walk is blameless.
O Lord Almighty, blessed is the man who
trusts in you.

PSALM 84:11-12 NIV

June 5

*B*e gracious to me, O God, according to Thy lovingkindness; according to the greatness of Thy compassion blot out my transgressions.

PSALM 51:1 NASB

June 6

Where can I go from your Spirit? Where can I flee from your presence? If I go up to the heavens, you are there; if I make my bed in the depths, you are there. If I rise on the wings of the dawn, if I settle on the far side of the sea, even there your hand will guide me, your right hand will hold me fast.

PSALM 139:7-10 NIV

June 7

Jesus said to him, "I am the way, the truth, and the life. No one comes to the Father except through Me."

JOHN 14:6 NKJV

June 8

God's love is meteoric, his loyalty astronomic, his purpose titanic, his verdicts oceanic. Yet in his largeness nothing gets lost.... How exquisite your love, O God! How eager we are to run under your wings.

PSALM 36:5-7 THE MESSAGE

June 9

But I pray to you, O Lord, in the time of your favor; in your great love, O God, answer me with your sure salvation.

PSALM 69:13 NIV

June 10

But as it is written, "What no eye has seen, nor ear heard, nor the human heart conceived, what God has prepared for those who love him"—these things God has revealed to us through the Spirit; for the Spirit searches everything, even the depths of God.

1 CORINTHIANS 2:9-10 NRSV

June 11

Your word, O Lord, is eternal; it stands firm
in the heavens. Your faithfulness continues through all
generations; you established the earth, and it endures.
Your laws endure to this day, for all things serve you.

PSALM 119:89-91 NIV

June 12

We can see and understand only a little about God now, as if we were peering at his reflection in a poor mirror; but someday we are going to see him in his completeness, face to face. Now all that I know is hazy and blurred, but then I will see everything clearly, just as clearly as God sees into my heart right now.

1 CORINTHIANS 13:12 TLB

June 13

All the paths of the Lord are mercy and truth,
to such as keep His covenant and His testimonies.

PSALM 25:10 NKJV

June 14

*H*e tends his flock like a shepherd: He gathers the lambs in his arms and carries them close to his heart; he gently leads those that have young.

ISAIAH 40:11 NIV

June 15

May Thy lovingkindnesses also come to me,
O Lord, Thy salvation according to Thy word.

Psalm 119:41 NASB

June 16

I am not ashamed, because I know whom I have
believed, and am convinced that he is able to guard
what I have entrusted to him for that day.

2 TIMOTHY 1:12 NIV

June 17

Be glad in the Lord and rejoice, O righteous, and shout for joy, all you upright in heart.

Psalm 32:11 NRSV

June 18

Because of the Lord's great love we are not consumed, for his compassions never fail. They are new every morning; great is your faithfulness.

LAMENTATIONS 3:22-23 NIV

June 19

Answer me quickly, O Lord; my spirit fails.
Do not hide your face from me, or I shall be like
those who go down to the Pit. Let me hear of your
steadfast love in the morning, for in you I put my trust.
Teach me the way I should go, for to you I
lift up my soul.

PSALM 143:7-8 NRSV

June 20

W

Wherever you go, I will go; and wherever
you lodge, I will lodge; your people shall be
my people, and your God, my God.

RUTH 1:16 NKJV

June 21

You know with all your heart and soul that not one of all the good promises the Lord your God gave you has failed. Every promise has been fulfilled; not one has failed.

JOSHUA 23:14 NIV

June 22

You will seek the Lord your God, and you will find him if you search after him with all your heart and soul.

DEUTERONOMY 4:29 NRSV

June 23

*A*s for God, his way is perfect; the word of the Lord is flawless. He is a shield for all who take refuge in him. For who is God besides the Lord? And who is the Rock except our God? It is God who arms me with strength and makes my way perfect.

2 SAMUEL 22:31-33 NIV

June 24

You are my God, and I will praise You; You are my God, I will exalt You. Oh, give thanks to the Lord, for He is good! For His mercy endures forever.

PSALM 118:28-29 NKJV

June 25

In peace I will both lie down and sleep, for Thou alone, O Lord, dost make me to dwell in safety.

PSALM 4:8 NASB

June 26

I will give you a new heart and put a new spirit in you; I will remove from you your heart of stone and give you a heart of flesh. And I will put my Spirit in you and move you to follow my decrees and be careful to keep my laws.

Ezekiel 36:26-27 niv

June 27

O Lord, you are our Father. We are the clay,
you are the potter; we are all the work of your hand.

ISAIAH 64:8 NIV

June 28

I will cause showers to come down in their season; there shall be showers of blessing.

EZEKIEL 34:26 NKJV

June 29

*N*ow faith is being sure of what we hope for and certain of what we do not see.

HEBREWS 11:1 NIV

June 30

*H*e sends from heaven and saves me... God sends his love and his faithfulness... Be exalted, O God, above the heavens; let your glory be over all the earth.

PSALM 57:3,5 NIV

July 1

*W*hom have I in heaven but you? And
there is nothing on earth that I desire other than you.
My flesh and my heart may fail but God is the
strength of my heart and my portion forever.

PSALM 73:25-26

July 2

$\mathcal{L}$et us draw near with a true heart in full assurance of faith, having our hearts sprinkled from an evil conscience and our bodies washed with pure water. Let us hold fast the confession of our hope without wavering, for He who promised is faithful.

HEBREWS 10:22-23 NKJV

July 3

*B*lessed be the God and Father of our Lord Jesus Christ, the Father of mercies and God of all comfort; who comforts us in all our affliction so that we may be able to comfort those who are in any affliction with the comfort with which we ourselves are comforted by God.

2 CORINTHIANS 1:3-4 NASB

July 4

My soul finds rest in God alone; my salvation comes from him. He alone is my rock and my salvation; he is my fortress, I will never be shaken... Find rest, O my soul, in God alone; my hope comes from him.

PSALM 62:1-2,5 NIV

July 5

He has made the earth by His power, He has established the world by His wisdom, and has stretched out the heavens at His discretion.

JEREMIAH 10:12 NRSV

July 6

*F*or it is by grace you have been saved, through faith—and this not from yourselves; it is the gift of God.

EPHESIANS 2:8 NIV

July 7

God isn't late with his promise as some measure
lateness. He is restraining himself on account
of you, holding back the End because he doesn't
want anyone lost. He's giving everyone space
and time to change.

2 PETER 3:9 THE MESSAGE

July 8

Behold, God is my salvation, I will trust and not be afraid; for the Lord God is my strength and song, and He has become my salvation.

ISAIAH 12:2 NASB

July 9

The Lord will guide you always; he will satisfy your needs in a sun-scorched land and will strengthen your frame. You will be like a well-watered garden, like a spring whose waters never fail.

ISAIAH 58:11 NIV

July 10

But He knows the way that I take; when He has tested me, I shall come forth as gold.

JOB 23:10 NKJV

July 11

As a father has compassion on his children, so the Lord has compassion on those who fear him; for he knows how we are formed, he remembers that we are dust. As for man, his days are like grass, he flourishes like a flower of the field.

PSALM 103:13-15 NIV

July 12

Real wisdom, God's wisdom, begins with a holy life and is characterized by getting along with others. It is gentle and reasonable, overflowing with mercy and blessings, not hot one day and cold the next, not two-faced.

JAMES 3:17 THE MESSAGE

July 13

$\mathcal{A}$nd whatever you do or say, let it be
as a representative of the Lord Jesus, and come
with him into the presence of God the Father
to give him your thanks.

COLOSSIANS 3:17 TLB

July 14

You will keep him in perfect peace, whose mind
is stayed on You, because he trusts in You.

ISAIAH 26:3 NKJV

July 15

May our Lord Jesus Christ himself and God our Father, who loved us and by his grace gave us eternal encouragement and good hope, encourage your hearts and strengthen you in every good deed and word.

2 Thessalonians 2:16-17 NIV

July 16

$\mathcal{Y}$ou prepare a table before me in the presence of my enemies; you anoint my head with oil; my cup overflows. Surely goodness and mercy shall follow me all the days of my life, and I shall dwell in the house of the Lord my whole life long.

PSALM 23:5-6 NRSV

July 17

As the deer pants for streams of water, so my soul pants for you, O God. My soul thirsts for God, for the living God. When can I go and meet with God?

PSALM 42:1-2 NIV

July 18

Therefore do not be like them; for your Father knows what you need, before you ask Him.

MATTHEW 6:8 NASB

July 19

Because you are my help, I sing in the shadow of your wings. My soul clings to you; your right hand upholds me.

PSALM 63:7-8 NIV

July 20

May his blessings and peace be yours, sent to you from God our Father and Jesus Christ our Lord. How we praise God... who has blessed us with every blessing in heaven because we belong to Christ. Long ago, even before he made the world, God chose us to be his very own through what Christ would do for us; he decided then to make us holy in his eyes, without a single fault—we who stand before him covered with his love.

EPHESIANS 1:2-4 TLB

July 21

*E*ach one should use whatever gift he has received to serve others, faithfully administering God's grace in its various forms.

1 PETER 4:10 NIV

July 22

When I look at your heavens, the work of your fingers, the moon and the stars that you have established; O Lord, our Sovereign, how majestic is your name in all the earth!

Psalm 8:3.9 NRSV

July 23

*F*or you created my inmost being; you knit me together in my mother's womb. I praise you because I am fearfully and wonderfully made; your works are wonderful, I know that full well.

PSALM 139:13-14 NIV

July 24

$\mathcal{L}$et those who boast, boast in this, that they understand and know me, that I am the Lord; I act with steadfast love, justice, and righteousness in the earth, for in these things I delight, says the Lord.

JEREMIAH 9:24 NRSV

July 25

There is nothing better for a man than to eat and drink and tell himself that his labor is good. This also I have seen, that it is from the hand of God. For who can eat and who can have enjoyment without Him? For to a person who is good in His sight He has given wisdom and knowledge and joy.

ECCLESIASTES 2:24-26 NASB

July 26

Since you have been chosen by God who has given you this new kind of life, and because of his deep love and concern for you, you should practice tenderhearted mercy and kindness to others. Don't worry about making a good impression on them, but be ready to suffer quietly and patiently. Be gentle and ready to forgive; never hold grudges. Remember, the Lord forgave you, so you must forgive others.

COLOSSIANS 3:12–13 TLB

July 27

*N*ow to the King eternal, immortal, invisible,
the only God, be honor and glory for ever
and ever. Amen.

1 TIMOTHY 1:17 NIV

July 28

From ages past no one has heard, no ear has perceived, no eye has seen any God besides you, who works for those who wait for him.

ISAIAH 64:4 NRSV

July 29

Oh come, let us worship and bow down; let us kneel before the Lord our Maker. For He is our God, and we are the people of His pasture, and the sheep of His hand.

PSALM 95:6-7 NKJV

July 30

The steadfast love of the Lord never ceases; his mercies never come to an end; they are new every morning; great is your faithfulness.

LAMENTATIONS 3:22–23 NRSV

July 31

You've been a safe place for me, a good place to hide.... I can always count on you—God, my dependable love.

PSALM 59:16-17 THE MESSAGE

August 1

Show me your ways, O Lord, teach me your
paths; guide me in your truth and teach me,
for you are God my Savior, and my hope is
in you all day long.

PSALM 25:4-5 NIV

August 2

Glory in His holy name; let the hearts of those rejoice who seek the Lord! Seek the Lord and His strength; seek His face evermore! Remember His marvelous works which He has done, His wonders, and the judgments of His mouth.

1 CHRONICLES 16:10–12 NKJV

August 3

"*With* everlasting kindness I will have compassion on you," says the Lord your Redeemer.

ISAIAH 54:8 NIV

August 4

$\mathcal{G}$od promises to love me all day, sing songs all through the night! My life is God's prayer.

PSALM 42:8 THE MESSAGE

August 5

$\mathcal{T}$hy kingdom is an everlasting kingdom, and Thy dominion endures throughout all generations. The eyes of all look to Thee, and Thou dost give them their food in due time. Thou dost open Thy hand, and dost satisfy the desire of every living thing.

PSALM 145:13,15-16 NASB

August 6

Yours, O Lord, is the greatness, the power and the glory, the victory and the majesty; for all that is in heaven and in earth is Yours; Yours is the kingdom, O Lord, and You are exalted as head over all.

1 CHRONICLES 29:11 NKJV

August 7

The Lord your God is with you... He will take great delight in you, he will quiet you with his love, he will rejoice over you with singing.

ZEPHANIAH 3:17 NIV

August 8

The mountains quake before him, and the hills melt; the earth heaves before him, the world and all who live in it. The Lord is good, a stronghold in a day of trouble; he protects those who take refuge in him.

NAHUM 1:5,7 NRSV

August 9

Satisfy us in the morning with your unfailing love, that we may sing for joy and be glad all our days.

PSALM 90:14 NIV

August 10

Embrace this God-life. Really embrace it, and nothing will be too much for you.... That's why I urge you to pray for absolutely everything, ranging from small to large. Include everything as you embrace this God-life, and you'll get God's everything.

MARK 11:22-24 THE MESSAGE

August 11

You in Your mercy have led forth the people whom You have redeemed; You have guided them in Your strength to Your holy habitation.

EXODUS 15:13 NKJV

August 12

The earth is the Lord's, and everything in it, the world, and all who live in it; for he founded it upon the seas and established it upon the waters.

PSALM 24:1-2 NIV

August 13

*A*bove all, keep fervent in your love for one another, because love covers a multitude of sins.

1 PETER 4:8 NASB

August 14

*G*od, who made the world and everything in it, since He is Lord of heaven and earth, does not dwell in temples made with hands. Nor is He worshiped with men's hands, as though He needed anything, since He gives to all life, breath, and all things.

ACTS 17:24–25 NKJV

August 15

$\mathcal{Y}$ou will keep in perfect peace him whose mind is steadfast, because he trusts in you. Trust in the Lord forever, for the Lord, the Lord, is the Rock eternal.

ISAIAH 26:3–4 NIV

August 16

*D*on't be afraid, for the Lord will go before
you and will be with you; he will not fail
nor forsake you.

DEUTERONOMY 31:8 TLB

August 17

Do you not know? Have you not heard? The Lord is the everlasting God, the Creator of the ends of the earth. He will not grow tired or weary, and his understanding no one can fathom.

ISAIAH 40:28 NIV

August 18

*F*or his anger is but for a moment; his favor is for a lifetime. Weeping may linger for the night, but joy comes with the morning.

PSALM 30:5 NRSV

August 19

I ask [God] that with both feet planted firmly on love, you'll be able to take in the extravagant dimensions of Christ's love. Reach out and experience the breadth! Test its length! Plumb the depths! Rise to the heights! Live full lives, full in the fullness of God. God can do anything, you know—far more than you could ever imagine or guess or request in your wildest dreams! He does it not by pushing us around but by working within us, his Spirit deeply and gently within us.

EPHESIANS 3:17-20 THE MESSAGE

August 20

If my people, who are called by my name, will humble themselves and pray and seek my face and turn from their wicked ways, then will I hear from heaven and will forgive their sin and will heal their land.

2 CHRONICLES 7:14 NIV

August 21

I call on you, O God, for you will answer me; give ear to me and hear my prayer. Show the wonder of your great love.... Keep me as the apple of your eye; hide me in the shadow of your wings.

PSALM 17:6-8 NIV

August 22

Do not withhold Your tender mercies from me,
O Lord; let Your lovingkindness and Your truth
continually preserve me.

Psalm 40:11 NKJV

August 23

For there is no difference between Jew and Gentile—
the same Lord is Lord of all and richly blesses all
who call on him.

ROMANS 10:12 NIV

August 24

This God—his way is perfect; the promise of the Lord proves true; he is a shield for all who take refuge in him.

PSALM 18:30 NRSV

August 25

*N*o one has seen God, ever. But if we love one another, God dwells deeply within us, and his love becomes complete in us—perfect love!

1 JOHN 4:12 THE MESSAGE

August 26

*B*e beautiful inside, in your hearts, with the lasting charm of a gentle and quiet spirit that is so precious to God.

1 PETER 3:4 TLB

August 27

*T*he Lord our God, the Lord is one. Love the Lord your God with all your heart and with all your soul and with all your mind and with all your strength.

MARK 12:29-30 NIV

August 28

*B*ut we have this treasure in earthen vessels, that the surpassing greatness of the power may be of God and not from ourselves.

2 CORINTHIANS 4:7 NASB

August 29

You are worthy, our Lord and God, to receive glory and honor and power, for you created all things, and by your will they were created and have their being.

REVELATION 4:11 NIV

August 30

Oh, what a wonderful God we have! How great are his wisdom and knowledge and riches! How impossible it is for us to understand his decisions and his methods! For who among us can know the mind of the Lord? Who knows enough to be his counselor and guide?

ROMANS 11:33-34 TLB

August 31

May God, who puts all things together, makes all things whole, now put you together, provide you with everything you need to please him, make us into what gives him most pleasure, by means of the sacrifice of Jesus, the Messiah. All glory to Jesus forever and always!

HEBREWS 13:20-21 THE MESSAGE

September 1

But Jesus looked at them and said, "With men it is impossible, but not with God; for with God all things are possible."

MARK 10:27 NKJV

September 2

*B*ut store up for yourselves treasures in heaven, where moth and rust do not destroy, and where thieves do not break in and steal. For where your treasure is, there your heart will be also.

MATTHEW 6:20-21 NIV

September 3

But the steadfast love of the Lord is from everlasting to everlasting on those who fear him, and his righteousness to children's children.

PSALM 103:17 NASB

September 4

*F*or he chose us in him before the creation of the world to be holy and blameless in his sight. In love he predestined us to be adopted as his sons through Jesus Christ, in accordance with his pleasure and will—to the praise of his glorious grace, which he has freely given us in the One he loves.

EPHESIANS 1:4-6 NIV

September 5

You're my place of quiet retreat; I wait for your Word to renew me therefore I lovingly embrace everything you say.

PSALM 119:114,119 THE MESSAGE

September 6

The Lord is my rock and my fortress and my deliverer, my God, my rock, in whom I take refuge; my shield and the horn of my salvation, my stronghold.

PSALM 18:2 NASB

September 7

Search me, O God, and know my heart; test me and know my anxious thoughts. See if there is any offensive way in me, and lead me in the way everlasting.

PSALM 139:23-24 NIV

September 8

The Lord shall preserve your going out and your coming in from this time forth, and even forevermore.

PSALM 121:8 NKJV

September 9

Bless the Lord, O my soul. O Lord my God, you are very great. You are clothed with honor and majesty, wrapped in light as with a garment. You stretch out the heavens like a tent, you set the beams of your chambers on the waters, you make the clouds your chariot, you ride on the wings of the wind. You set the earth on its foundations, so that it shall never be shaken.

PSALM 104:1-3,5 NRSV

September 10

$\mathcal{B}$lessed are those who are persecuted because
of righteousness, for theirs is the kingdom of heaven.

MATTHEW 5:10 NIV

September 11

Call to Me, and I will answer you, and
I will tell you great and mighty things, which
you do not know.

Jeremiah 33:3 NASB

September 12

$\mathcal{T}$his is the kind of love we are talking about—not that we once upon a time loved God, but that he loved us and sent his Son as a sacrifice to clear away our sins and the damage they've done to our relationship with God. My dear, dear friends, if God loved us like this, we certainly ought to love each other.

1 JOHN 4:10-11 THE MESSAGE

September 13

*D*on't worry about anything; instead, pray about everything; tell God your needs, and don't forget to thank him for his answers.

PHILIPPIANS 4:6 TLB

September 14

Thus says the Lord, he who created you..., "I have called you by name, you are mine. When you pass through the waters, I will be with you; and through the rivers, they shall not overwhelm you."

ISAIAH 43:1-2 NRSV

September 15

Deep calls to deep in the roar of your waterfalls;
all your waves and breakers have swept over me. By
day the Lord directs his love, at night his song
is with me—a prayer to the God of my life.

PSALM 42:7-8 NIV

September 16

I have loved you with an everlasting love;
therefore I have continued my faithfulness to you.

JEREMIAH 31:3 NRSV

September 17

The fulfillment of God's promise depends entirely on trusting God and his way, and then simply embracing him and what he does. God's promise arrives as pure gift.

ROMANS 4:16 THE MESSAGE

September 18

God is able to make all grace abound to you, so that in all things at all times, having all that you need, you will abound in every good work.

2 CORINTHIANS 9:8 NIV

September 19

*N*o wonder we are happy in the Lord! For we
are trusting him. We trust his holy name. Yes, Lord,
let your constant love surround us, for our hopes are
in you alone.

PSALM 33:21-22 TLB

September 20

The Lord is gracious and merciful, slow to anger and abounding in steadfast love. The Lord is good to all, and his compassion is over all that he has made.... The Lord is faithful in all his words, and gracious in all his deeds.

PSALM 145:8–9,13 NRSV

September 21

*W*ith the Lord a day is like a thousand years,
and a thousand years are like a day. The Lord is not
slow in keeping his promise, as some understand
slowness. He is patient with you.

2 PETER 3:8-9 NIV

September 22

Your heavenly Father knows your needs. He will always give you all you need from day to day.

LUKE 12:30-31 TLB

September 23

For all God's words are right, and everything he does is worthy of our trust. He loves whatever is just and good; the earth is filled with his tender love. He merely spoke, and the heavens were formed, and all the galaxies of stars. He made the oceans, pouring them into his vast reservoirs.

PSALM 33:4–7 TLB

September 24

I am convinced that neither death, nor life, nor angels, nor rulers, nor things present, nor things to come, nor powers, nor height, nor depth, nor anything else in all creation, will be able to separate us from the love of God.

ROMANS 8:38–39 NRSV

September 25

$\mathcal{I}$ will betroth you to Me forever; yes, I will betroth you to Me in righteousness and justice, in lovingkindness and mercy; I will betroth you to Me in faithfulness, and you shall know the Lord.

HOSEA 2:19-20 NKJV

September 26

I am the vine; you are the branches. If a man remains in me and I in him, he will bear much fruit; apart from me you can do nothing.

JOHN 15:5 NIV

September 27

*F*or the soul of every living thing is in the hand of God, and the breath of all mankind.

JOB 12:10 TLB

September 28

The Lord is slow to anger and great in power....
His way is in the whirlwind and the storm, and
clouds are the dust of his feet.

NAHUM 1:3 NIV

September 29

Set your minds on things that are above, not on things that are on earth, for you have died, and your life is hidden with Christ in God. When Christ who is your life is revealed, then you also will be revealed with him in glory.

COLOSSIANS 3:2-4 NRSV

September 30

These things I have spoken to you, that My joy may be in you, and that your joy may be made full. This is My commandment, that you love one another, just as I have loved you. Greater love has no one than this, that one lay down his life for his friends.

JOHN 15:11-13 NASB

October 1

You know me inside and out...You know exactly how I was made, bit by bit, how I was sculpted from nothing into something. Like an open book, you watched me grow from conception to birth; all the stages of my life were spread out before you before I'd even lived one day.

PSALM 139:15-16 THE MESSAGE

October 2

$\mathcal{F}$or with you is the fountain of life; in your light we see light. Continue your love to those who know you, your righteousness to the upright in heart.

PSALM 36:9-10 NIV

October 3

I love the Lord because he hears my prayers and answers them. Because he bends down and listens, I will pray as long as I breathe!

PSALM 116:1-2 TLB

October 4

The righteous cry out, and the Lord hears them;
he delivers them from all their troubles. The Lord
is close to the brokenhearted and saves those who
are crushed in spirit.

PSALM 34:17-18 NIV

October 5

"O give thanks to the Lord, for he is good; for his steadfast love endures forever." Say also: "Save us, O God of our salvation, and gather and rescue us from among the nations, that we may give thanks to your holy name, and glory in your praise. Blessed be the Lord, the God of Israel, from everlasting to everlasting." Then all the people said "Amen!" and praised the Lord.

1 CHRONICLES 16:34-36 NRSV

October 6

Ascribe to the Lord the glory due his name;
worship the Lord in the splendor of his holiness.
The voice of the Lord is over the waters; the God
of glory thunders; the Lord thunders over the mighty
waters. The voice of the Lord is powerful; the voice
of the Lord is majestic.

PSALM 29:2-4 NIV

October 7

$\mathcal{M}$ay the God of hope fill you with all joy and peace as you trust in him, so that you may overflow with hope.

ROMANS 15:13 NIV

October 8

The basic reality of God is plain enough. Open your eyes and there it is! By taking a long and thoughtful look at what God has created, people have always been able to see what their eyes as such can't see: eternal power, for instance, and the mystery of his divine being.

ROMANS 1:19-20 THE MESSAGE

October 9

*C*reate in me a pure heart, O God, and renew a steadfast spirit within me....The sacrifices of God are a broken spirit; a broken and contrite heart, O God, you will not despise.

PSALM 51:10,17 NIV

October 10

$\mathcal{A}$nd all these blessings shall come upon you and overtake you, because you obey the voice of the Lord your God.

DEUTERONOMY 28:2 NKJV

October 11

God's peace...is far more wonderful than the human mind can understand. His peace will keep your thoughts and your hearts quiet and at rest.

PHILIPPIANS 4:7 TLB

October 12

Dear children, let us not love with words or tongue but with actions and in truth. This then is how we know that we belong to the truth, and how we set our hearts at rest in his presence... For God is greater than our hearts, and he knows everything.

1 JOHN 3:18-20 NIV

October 13

*D*o you not know that those who run in a race all run, but one receives the prize? Run in such a way that you obtain *it*. And everyone who competes *for the prize* is temperate in all things. Now they *do it* to obtain a perishable crown, but we *for* an imperishable crown. Therefore I run thus: not with uncertainty.

1 CORINTHIANS 9:24-26 NKJV

October 14

You're blessed when you care. At the moment of being "care-full" you find yourselves cared for. You're blessed when you get your inside world— your mind and heart—put right. Then you can see God in the outside world.

MATTHEW 5:7-8 THE MESSAGE

October 15

*B*ut when you pray, go into your room, close
the door and pray to your Father, who is unseen.
Then your Father, who sees what is done in secret,
will reward you.

MATTHEW 6:6 NIV

October 16

Thus says the Lord, who created you, O Jacob, and He who formed you, O Israel: "Fear not, for I have redeemed you; I have called you by your name; you are Mine. When you pass through the waters, I will be with you; and through the rivers, they shall not overflow you. When you walk through the fire, you shall not be burned, nor shall the flame scorch you.

ISAIAH 43:1-2 NKJV

October 17

God, who knows the heart, bore witness to the Gentiles, giving them the Holy Spirit, just as He also did to the Jews; and He made no distinction between us and them, cleansing their hearts by faith... We believe that we are saved through the grace of the Lord Jesus.

ACTS 15:8-9,11 NASB

October 18

The Lord is righteous in all his ways and loving toward all he has made. The Lord is near to all who call on him, to all who call on him in truth. He fulfills the desires of those who fear him; he hears their cry and saves them.

PSALM 145:17-19 NIV

October 19

So let us come boldly to the very throne of God and stay there to receive his mercy and to find grace to help us in our times of need.

HEBREWS 4:16 TLB

October 20

Our mouths were filled with laughter, our tongues with songs of joy. Then it was said among the nations, "The Lord has done great things for them." The Lord has done great things for us, and we are filled with joy.

PSALM 126:1-3 NIV

October 21

You've always been great toward me—what love...
You, O God, are both tender and kind, not easily
angered, immense in love, and you never, never quit.

PSALM 86:13,15 THE MESSAGE

October 22

$\mathcal{B}$ut I will sing of your strength; in the morning I will sing of your love; for you are my fortress, my refuge in times of trouble. O my Strength, I sing praise to you; you, O God, are my fortress, my loving God.

PSALM 59:16-17 NIV

October 23

Even to your old age and gray hairs I am he,
I am he who will sustain you. I have made you
and I will carry you; I will sustain you
and I will rescue you.

ISAIAH 46:4 NIV

October 24

$\mathcal{B}$y day the Lord directs his love, at night his song is with me—a prayer to the God of my life.

PSALM 42:8 NIV

October 25

For the love of Christ urges us on, because we are convinced that one has died for all; therefore all have died. And he died for all, so that those who live might live no longer for themselves, but for him who died and was raised for them.

2 CORINTHIANS 5:14-15 NRSV

October 26

*P*leasant words are a honeycomb, sweet to the
soul and healing to the bones.

PROVERBS 16:24 NIV

October 27

Why is everyone hungry for more?... I have God's more-than-enough, more joy in one ordinary day.... At day's end I'm ready for sound sleep, for you, God, have put my life back together.

PSALM 4:6-8 THE MESSAGE

October 28

Since what may be known about God is plain to them, because God has made it plain to them. For since the creation of the world God's invisible qualities—his eternal power and divine nature—have been clearly seen, being understood from what has been made, so that men are without excuse.

ROMANS 1:19-20 NIV

October 29

The Spirit of God has made me, and the breath of the Almighty gives me life... Behold, I belong to God like you, I too have been formed out of the clay.

JOB 33:4,6 NASB

October 30

$\mathcal{J}$esus said to the disciples, "If you only have faith in God—this is the absolute truth—you can say to this Mount of Olives, 'Rise up and fall into the Mediterranean,' and your command will be obeyed. All that's required is that you really believe and have no doubt!"

MARK 11:22-23 TLB

October 31

Can you fathom the mysteries of God? Can you probe the limits of the Almighty? They are higher than the heavens—what can you do? They are deeper than the depths of the grave—what can you know? Their measure is longer than the earth and wider than the sea.

JOB 11:7-9 NIV

November 1

Satisfy us in the morning with your steadfast love, so that we may rejoice and be glad all our days.

PSALM 90:14 NRSV

November 2

Live out your God-created identity. Live generously and graciously toward others, the way God lives toward you.

MATTHEW 5:48 THE MESSAGE

November 3

*F*or I have satiated the weary soul, and I have replenished every sorrowful soul.

JEREMIAH 31:25 NKJV

November 4

Therefore, the promise comes by faith, so that it may be by grace and may be guaranteed to all Abraham's offspring—not only to those who are of the law but also to those who are of the faith of Abraham. He is the father of us all.

ROMANS 4:16 NIV

November 5

*A*nd why do you worry about clothing?
Consider the lilies of the field, how they grow; they
neither toil nor spin, yet I tell you, even Solomon in all
his glory was not clothed like one of these. But if God
so clothes the grass of the field, which is alive today
and tomorrow is thrown into the oven, will he not
much more clothe you—you of little faith?

MATTHEW 6:28-30 NRSV

November 6

$\mathcal{B}$ut he who is greatest among you shall be your servant. And whoever exalts himself will be humbled, and he who humbles himself will be exalted.

MATTHEW 23:11-12 NKJV

November 7

Give thanks to the Lord, for he is good. His love endures forever. Give thanks to the God of gods. His love endures forever. Give thanks to the Lord of lords: His love endures forever. To him who alone does great wonders, his love endures forever.

PSALM 136:1–4 NIV

November 8

You own the day, you own the night; you put stars
and sun in place. You laid out the four corners
of earth, shaped the seasons of summer and winter.

PSALM 74:16-17 THE MESSAGE

November 9

*M*ay God be gracious to us and bless us and make his face shine upon us, that your ways may be known on earth, your salvation among all nations.

PSALM 67:1-2 NIV

November 10

If you love someone, you will be loyal to him no matter what the cost. You will always believe in him, always expect the best of him, and always stand your ground in defending him.... Love goes on forever.

1 CORINTHIANS 13:7–8 TLB

November 11

Yours is the day, yours also the night; you
established the luminaries and the sun. You have
fixed all the bounds of the earth; you
made summer and winter.

PSALM 74:16-17 NRSV

November 12

The Lord is gracious and compassionate, slow to anger and rich in love. The Lord is good to all; he has compassion on all he has made.

PSALM 145:8-9 NIV

November 13

*A*nd what is it that God has said? That he
has given us eternal life and that this life is in his Son.
So whoever has God's Son has life; whoever does not
have his Son, does not have life.

1 JOHN 5:11-12 TLB

November 14

*U*ntil now you have not asked for anything
in my name. Ask and you will receive,
and your joy will be complete.

JOHN 16:24 NIV

November 15

Steep yourself in God-reality, God-initiative, God-provisions. You'll find all your everyday human concerns will be met. Don't be afraid of missing out. You're my dearest friends! The Father wants to give you the very kingdom itself.

LUKE 12:28 THE MESSAGE

November 16

Jesus answered and said to him, "If anyone loves Me, he will keep My word; and My Father will love him, and We will come to him, and make Our abode with him."

JOHN 14:23 NASB

November 17

l cry aloud to the Lord; I lift up my voice to the Lord for mercy.... When my spirit grows faint within me, it is you who know my way.

PSALM 142:1-3 NIV

November 18

*There is one God, and there is no other but He.
And to love Him with all the heart, with all the
understanding, with all the soul, and with all the
strength, and to love one's neighbor as oneself, is more
than all the whole burnt offerings and sacrifices.*

MARK 12:32-33 NKJV

November 19

*B*ut you are a chosen race, a royal priesthood, a holy nation, God's own people, in order that you may proclaim the mighty acts of him who called you out of darkness into his marvelous light.

1 PETER 2:9 NRSV

November 20

Do you want to stand out? Then step down. Be a servant. If you puff yourself up, you'll get the wind knocked out of you. But if you're content to simply be yourself, your life will count for plenty.

MATTHEW 23:11-12 THE MESSAGE

November 21

$\mathcal{Y}$our kingdom come, your will be done on
earth as it is in heaven.

MATTHEW 6:10 NIV

November 22

For you, O Lord, have made me glad by your work; at the works of your hands I sing for joy. How great are your works, O Lord! Your thoughts are very deep!

PSALM 92:4-5 NRSV

November 23

$\mathcal{A}$nd the God of all grace, who called you
to his eternal glory in Christ, after you have suffered
a little while, will himself restore you and make
you strong, firm and steadfast.

1 PETER 5:10 NIV

$\mathcal{N}$ovember 24

*K*now also that wisdom is sweet to your soul; if you find it, there is a future hope for you, and your hope will not be cut off.

PROVERBS 24:14 NIV

November 25

$\mathcal{T}$his is my prayer: that your love will flourish and
that you will not only love much but well. Learn to
love appropriately. You need to use your head
and test your feelings so that your love is sincere
and intelligent, not sentimental gush.

PHILIPPIANS 1:9-10 THE MESSAGE

November 26

*T*wo are better than one, because they have a good reward for their toil. For if they fall one will lift up the other.

ECCLESIASTES 4:9-10 NRSV

November 27

Cling to wisdom—she will protect you. Love her—she will guard you. Getting wisdom is the most important thing you can do! And with your wisdom, develop common sense and good judgment.

PROVERBS 4:6-7 TLB

November 28

*M*y child, do not let these escape from your sight keep sound wisdom and prudence, and they will be life for your soul and adornment for your neck.

PROVERBS 3:21-22 NRSV

November 29

*N*o eye has seen, nor ear heard, nor the human
heart conceived, what God has prepared
for those who love him.

1 CORINTHIANS 2:9 NRSV

November 30

Praise be to the Lord, for he has heard my cry for mercy. The Lord is my strength and my shield; my heart trusts in him, and I am helped. My heart leaps for joy and I will give thanks to him in song.

PSALM 28:6-77 NIV

December 1

$\mathcal{P}$ursue a righteous life—a life of wonder, faith, love, steadiness, courtesy. Run hard and fast in the faith. Seize the eternal life, the life you were called to.

1 TIMOTHY 6:11-12 THE MESSAGE

December 2

*H*e has given us his very great and precious promises.... For this very reason, make every effort to add to your faith goodness; and to goodness, knowledge; and to knowledge, self-control; and to self-control, perseverance; and to perseverance, godliness.

2 PETER 1:4-6 NIV

December 3

In everything you do, put God first, and he will direct you and crown your efforts with success.

PROVERBS 3:6 TLB

December 4

If any of you lacks wisdom, he should ask God, who gives generously to all without finding fault, and it will be given to him. But when he asks, he must believe and not doubt, because he who doubts is like a wave of the sea, blown and tossed by the wind.

JAMES 1:5-6 NIV

December 5

The Lord will keep you from all harm—he will watch over your life; the Lord will watch over your coming and going both now and forevermore.

PSALM 121:7-8 NIV

December 6

A wise person gets known for insight; gracious words add to one's reputation.

PROVERBS 16:21 THE MESSAGE

December 7

$\mathcal{T}$hen I lay down and slept in peace and woke up safely, for the Lord was watching over me. And now, although ten thousand enemies surround me on every side, I am not afraid.

PSALM 3:5-6 TLB

December 8

The Lord is gracious and full of compassion, slow
to anger and great in mercy.

PSALM 145:8 NKJV

December 9

*H*ow many are your works, O Lord!
In wisdom you made them all; the earth is full of
your creatures.... These all look to you to give them
their food at the proper time.... May the glory
of the Lord endure forever; may the Lord
rejoice in his works.

PSALM 104:24,27,31 NIV

December 10

Praise the Lord, O my soul; all my inmost being,
praise his holy name. Praise the Lord, O my soul, and
forget not all his benefits.

PSALM 103:1-2 NIV

December 11

Jesus responded, "The real significance of that Scripture is not that Moses gave you bread from heaven but that my Father is right now offering you bread from heaven, the real bread. The Bread of God came down out of heaven and is giving life to the world."

JOHN 6:32-33 THE MESSAGE

December 12

$\mathcal{L}$et them give thanks to the Lord for his unfailing
love... for he satisfies the thirsty and fills the hungry
with good things.

PSALM 107:8-9 NIV

December 13

*F*or God alone my soul waits in silence; from him comes my salvation. He alone is my rock and my salvation, my fortress; I shall never be shaken.

PSALM 62:1-2 NRSV

December 14

And you, my child, will be called a prophet of the Most High; for you will go on before the Lord to prepare the way for him, to give his people the knowledge of salvation through the forgiveness of their sins, because of the tender mercy of our God, by which the rising sun will come to us from heaven to shine on those living in darkness and in the shadow of death, to guide our feet into the path of peace.

LUKE 1:76-79 NIV

December 15

$\mathcal{L}$ove the Lord your God with all your heart and with all your soul and with all your strength.

DEUTERONOMY 6:5 NIV

December 16

Isn't everything you have and everything you are sheer gifts from God?... You already have all you need.

1 CORINTHIANS 4:7-8 THE MESSAGE

December 17

$\mathcal{G}$ive generously, for your gifts will return to you later.... It is a wonderful thing to be alive! If a person lives to be very old, let him rejoice in every day of life, but let him also remember that eternity is far longer and that everything down here is futile in comparison.

ECCLESIASTES 11:1,7-8 TLB

December 18

*R*emember the words of the Lord Jesus, that He said, "It is more blessed to give than to receive."

ACTS 20:35 NKJV

December 19

The Word became flesh and made his dwelling among us. We have seen his glory, the glory of the One and Only, who came from the Father, full of grace and truth.

JOHN 1:14 NIV

December 20

We all live off his generous bounty, gift after gift after gift. We got the basics from Moses, and then this exuberant giving and receiving, this endless knowing and understanding—all this came through Jesus, the Messiah.

JOHN 1:16-17 THE MESSAGE

December 21

Give away your life; you'll find life given back,
but not merely given back—given back with bonus and
blessing. Giving, not getting, is the way. Generosity
begets generosity.

LUKE 6:38 THE MESSAGE

December 22

And the Word became flesh, and dwelt among us, and we beheld His glory, glory as of the only begotten from the Father, full of grace and truth.

JOHN 1:14 NASB

December 23

"Behold, the virgin shall be with child, and bear a Son and they shall call His name Immanuel," which is translated, "God with us."

MATTHEW 1:23 NKJV

December 24

For to us a child is born, to us a son is given, and the government will be on his shoulders. And he will be called Wonderful Counselor, Mighty God, Everlasting Father, Prince of Peace.

ISAIAH 9:6 NIV

December 25

$\mathcal{T}$hanks be to God for His indescribable gift!

2 CORINTHIANS 9:15 NKJV

December 26

$\mathcal{A}$rise, shine, for your light has come, and the glory of the Lord rises upon you. See, darkness covers the earth and thick darkness is over the peoples, but the Lord rises upon you and his glory appears over you.

ISAIAH 60:1-2 NIV

December 27

For Thou, O Lord, hast made me glad by what Thou hast done, I will sing for joy at the works of Thy hands. How great are Thy works, O Lord! Thy thoughts are very deep.

PSALM 92:4-5 NASB

December 28

*T*he law of the Lord is perfect, reviving the soul. The statutes of the Lord are trustworthy, making wise the simple. The precepts of the Lord are right, giving joy to the heart. The commands of the Lord are radiant, giving light to the eyes. The fear of the Lord is pure, enduring forever. The ordinances of the Lord are sure and altogether righteous.

PSALM 19:7-9 NIV

December 29

As obedient children, let yourselves be pulled into a way of life shaped by God's life, a life energetic and blazing with holiness.... Your life is a journey you must travel with a deep consciousness of God.

1 PETER 1:15,17 THE MESSAGE

December 30

$\mathcal{M}$ay the Lord continually bless you
with heaven's blessings as well as with human joys.

PSALM 128:5 TLB

December 31